When You're Tired of LOOKING UP

...Because nothing GOOD seems to be falling into your life!

By

Gladys Henderson-Williams

This book is a work of non-fiction. Names and places have been changed to protect the privacy of all individuals. The events and situations are true.

© 2003 by Gladys Henderson-Williams. All rights reserved.

No part of this book may be reproduced, stored in a retrieval system, or transmitted by any means, electronic, mechanical, photocopying, recording, or otherwise, without written permission from the author.

ISBN: 1-4107-4567-8 (e-book)
ISBN: 1-4107-4566-X (Paperback)

Library of Congress Control Number: 2003093246

This book is printed on acid free paper.

Printed in the United States of America
Bloomington, IN

1stBooks - rev. 7/18/03

.... *what people are saying*

One of the greatest experiences we can have is to encounter people who possess a perspective on life that both positively challenge and change us when we hear them. This is exactly what "When You're Tired Of Looking Up" accomplishes as access is granted into issues of the heart that people struggle with daily. The pinnacle is a realization that God's eternal plan ensures a safe arrival at your destiny, even through life's most fierce storms.

Gerard H. Ruff
Sr. Pastor Cornerstone Assembly of God Church
Hampton, Virginia

Due to my hectic schedule as a sophomore at Norfolk State University, I have very little time for reading for enjoyment but once I began reading "When You're Tired Of Looking Up" I was unable to put it down. The book was so interesting and captivating that I read it in one night. The author explained the meaning of "Manifest Destiny" better than any history class I have ever taken. As a young adult, I found the book easy to understand. The author was very skillful in writing in such a manner that no matter what age or stage you are in you will be able to relate to her personal pathway to a closer relationship with God. The author was very explicit in revealing the struggle you can encounter as a Christian but she was equally *encouraging that we should never give up until we have reached our goal. I would highly recommend this book to teenagers and young adults with the hope that we can learn from the author's experience and our road to "Manifest Destiny" may not be as hard. Thank you for a wonderful road map.*

Aja Williams
Daughter, Andrew Williams and Gladys Henderson-Williams
Sophomore Norfolk State University
Norfolk, Virginia

I believe this book will help transmogrify the lives of all readers that desire a greater depth in God. Gladys' openness and honesty allows one to see the mercy, love and grace of God. In the Christian walk with God, sometimes stumbling, confused, heart broken and eyes blinded with tears, causes many to experience the faithfulness of God. This book shows that God is the author and finisher of our faith, with a preordained destiny. Thank you, Gladys, for being transparent; only a true leader will share the intimacy and process that it takes in making a good leader. I applaud you for birthing the knowledge in ink of a long awaited book.

Dr. Ruby L. Pedescleaux
Sr. Pastor, Showers of Blessing Ministries
Shreveport, Louisiana

Inspirational, informational, but most importantly, transformational, are the adjectives that come to mind to describe this book. God certainly has used the God-directed experiences of this author to bless the readers. Though we all have our own paths to follow, journeys to travel, lessons to learn and destinies to fulfill, this book helps to give us some spiritual guidance through the maze and daze that we all can often find ourselves. This publication assists us in understanding that our experiences (pleasant or unpleasant) are not always understood by family, friends, fellow church members, or even the pastor, but God knows how to orchestrate us through certain trials, unsuspected changes, painful tribulations and abrupt shifts in our lives. After all, He is the One who purposed and designed our ultimate destination and knows just what He is doing to eventually get us to where He wants us to be. This book will help you to realize and reach the "Manifest Destiny" He has for you.

Dr. Marcia Banks-Alston
Author: "How We Are Being Tricked and Bamboozled into Bad Health"

From the first page of this book, I found myself drawn into the author's quest for a clearer understanding of who God is. I believe, as does the author, that if we truly desire to know where God is taking us, He (God) will enlighten us. Gladys Henderson does what only

Gladys Henderson can do: DEMAND YOUR ATTENTION UNTIL SHE'S FINISHED SPEAKING. This writing presents the body of Christ with a much needed realness. Many of us who have deemed ourselves as "Spiritual Giants" (so We say) have said the same thing, "I am tired of looking up and nothing seems to be falling," but Gladys Henderson, in her book, is one of few people who are willing and bold enough to share it with others and provide personal examples of how to hold on until your Manifest Destiny becomes a reality. This book is a wonderful resource for any person who desires an honest look at how and what following the ways of the Lord may involve. Great Read! Thanks Gladys for your BOLDNESS.

Dorothy Govan, M.Div
Pastor, Progressive Life in Christ Ministry
Hampton, Virginia

DEDICATION

This book is dedicated to my loving and supportive husband, Andrew Jonathan Williams Sr. You believed in me even when I didn't believe in me, thanks. To my parents Rev. Paul Colwell (deceased) and Iola "Ola" Colwell. My sisters, Ruth Wallace (deceased), Dorothy King (deceased) miss you girls, and Inez Ann Fluker. To all my children, Neco, Tatanashe (Chocolate), Jai-Keith, Andrew Jr., Aja, Shaun, Rodney, Tina, and Rekinna. My Sweetie, Booptie, Nich, and the Louisiana connection. Thanks for believing in me throughout the years. Without your encouragement this book would not have been accomplished.

ACKNOWLEDGEMENTS

My Family:

Paul and Iola Colwell – Preacher and Teacher, a beautiful team for 50 years, Ruth, Dorothy and Ann - Ruth-strength; Dorothy-friend; Ann-our baby

Andrew J. Williams Sr. - "my bestest friend"

Neco & Sheila - "quiet strength"

Chocolate & Carlos - "anchored and anointed"

Jai-Keith "Uncle Keefee" - "focused"

Andrew Jr. "Uncle 2-Lu" – "compassionate"

Aja - "anointed and determined"

Shaun – "humble"

Rodney – Dunnie –"preacher man"

Louisiana Connection : Tina, Rekinna and the magnificent seven

Dr. Ruby Lee Pedescleaux

Thanks for the impartation and not giving up on your cuz. Love you much.

Dr. Rita Twiggs.

A true mentor and teacher. Thanks for letting me serve.

Senior Pastors Gerard and Kimberly Ruff

"The Mentality of a Visionary"- Thanks for your encouragement and taking the time to write a review.

Mrs. Violet Williams Gray
   The best mother-in-law in the world. Thanks for your baby.

Pastor Lawrence and Dorothy Govan
   What can I say? Thanks for letting me drop in at any time and disturb your church meetings.

Mrs. Cheryl Camm
   My (adopted) sister. Thanks for helping to take care of momma.

Bishop Clyde and Marsha Nichols
   Thanks for being true friends. My Denver Pastor and President of the 1st Ladies Council

Pastor Arthur and Cindy Groomes
   Look where God has brought us?

Deacon Joseph Williams Jr., Deacon Peter Williams, Bae-Bae, Ann and Janice
   Thanks for accepting me into the family.

Minister Jada E. Jackson

My Friend, My Editor, My Prayer partner, My sister, the list is too long. Thanks girl for all the late night talks. I owe you girl.

Elder Dr. Barbara and Deacon Anderson

My confidant and friends. Thanks for letting me escape to your home for some much needed rest.

Dr. Marcia and Mr. Rodney Alston

Friendship is important and I value ours greatly

Mr. Allen and Mrs. Paulette Jones

My Washington DC Editor. Keen eyes are so important to have, thanks. You 2 Jeremy

Mr. Ellis and Betty Shepherd and the Angelic Gospel Chorus

My homies – I will never out grow home. Thanks for your love.

The Mighty Women's Ministry of Cornerstone

All 250 strong – Thanks for letting me be me. God's gonna bless you for putting up with me for 10 years. Luv – U All

Gifted Hands

Barbara Mouring, Linda Ann Alston, Arlene Cofield. Valerie Twine, Betty "Boo" Jones, Carolyn Bonds, and the two Dr(s). Thanks for believing in me.

My church family

To all of the departments and auxiliaries, thanks for your continued encouragement, especially the Men's Ministry.

Encouragers:

Melvin (my buddy) and Merel Mills! Rev. Tim and Evangelist Dee Bell! Pastor Lena Mae Alston! Terry and Gail Banks-Taylor – a rock! Co-workers, Babs, Johnny, Van, Reginna, Lashecco, Mabel, Colonel Deborah Bielling and General Larry and Mrs. Ora Spencer! Jamelle "Ceasarette" Mason! Ty Banks – thanks for fixing my computer! Dorothy Robinson, Pastor Shirley Lancaster, Dorothy Johnson (Ms. Dot), Johnnie Lloyd, and whomever I've forgotten to thank—I love you 2!

PREFACE

It has been my pleasure to have known Mrs. Gladys Henderson-Williams for the past 10 years. She is a wonderful and committed Christian woman who devotes her time and talents uplifting the Kingdom of God. She is a dedicated wife, mother, professional financial manager and Spiritual leader who has written a wonderful inspirational book with a message for the ages.

As its core, this book challenges us all to examine our relationship with our Savior, Jesus Christ. She eloquently makes the point that simply looking up for "manna from Heaven" is not the answer...the answer is a real and sincere relationship with Christ. She stresses that simply going through the motions of being a Christian profits us little-in the end, we must know that we know that Jesus is the living Son of God and his Love is everlasting.

A powerful message such as this would easily satisfy the needs of most readers; however, Gladys takes a bold step and craftily weaves in personal experiences and testimonies that really bring this message to life. From her devoted father to personal mentors and teachers, Gladys provides insight into her personal journey along her Christian walk. She also reveals the personal tragedy involving her sister that led to a life-altering experience at the altar. Finally, Gladys speaks lovingly about her relationship with her children and the dedication and love of her husband.

In short, "When You're Tired of Looking Up" is a powerful message that is relevant today and tomorrow. It's a message that you will want to read over and over again. It will challenge you to seek out a personal relationship with Christ while providing the assurance that despite all of the knocks in life, Christ loves us and seeks our love.

Brigadier General Larry Spencer
United States Air Force

INTRODUCTION

Wow! How did you know that—you must be a prophet, with that great voice you should record a CD, you can chair the Trustee Board just as good as he can, why don't you start your own church? Day in and day out we are constantly bombarded with these types of statements only to realize we don't have a clue of what God has destined for our lives.

Many times we wander aimlessly through life trying to find the answer to a question that has plagued every Christian at one time or another; what is my destiny and how do I achieve it? We continue to find ourselves at the same old crossroads asking the same old questions—where do I go from here? Lord, what would you have me to do? Lord, what is <u>my</u> ministry? You know the questions I'm referring to. After awhile, we get so frustrated that we begin to seek counsel from our friends, relatives, co-workers, or pastors. We'll ask anyone that we feel can give us the answer we need, praying that someone, anyone would shed some light on that ever darkening, bleak subject called "DESTINY". Finally we hear "that word" from God through a person and we know that this is "it", this is what God has called us to do and we set out on the journey.

Although we are aspiring for this goal, something still doesn't feel right—-hmm I wonder what it could be? You are right; this is not God's plan for your life. It might be a fine plan, one that will yield a harvest, but it is not God's ultimate destiny for your life.

In this book, I will share with you some precious truths that God has revealed to me on how to achieve your destiny. I will first attempt to explain what God revealed to me about the meaning of destiny. Most of us feel like it is a fine house, a great job, a wonderful spouse, obedient kids and the list is endless. Please don't misunderstand me, those things can definitely be attained as a part of reaching your final destiny, but what God has shown me is that He wants "YOU". The army says Uncle Sam wants you, but God wants you totally committed to Him no matter what the circumstance. He wants a relationship with you that will withstand the test of time.

Walk with me down the long winding path that led me to my destiny. The road was extremely rocky at times and the valleys were oh so deep, but I was determined to at least get a glimpse of what God's plan was for my life. I pray as you read this book you will let the Lord minister to your spirit and either confirm that you are on the right road or reveal the road map that will lead you to your own personal destiny.

May God Bless You
Gladys Henderson-Williams

Now unto Him that is able to keep you from falling, and to present you faultless before the presences of his glory with exceeding great joy, to the only wise God our Saviour, be glory and majesty, dominion and power, both now and forever. Amen

Jude 24-25

CHAPTER ONE
LOOKING FOR DESTINY
IN ALL THE
WRONG PLACES

When I was a teenager, I was taught in History Class about something called "Manifest Destiny." I wondered why I needed to know about a US policy of imperative expansion that happened in the 19th and early 20th century. Who cares? To this day, I have had no use for the fact that I studied something about Manifest Destiny! It was not until I began writing this book, however, that I realized Manifest Destiny also means "future event regarded as unavoidable."

Some of us begin our lives facing innumerable obstacles. These obstacles may possibly have included the absence of a parent, financial needs, inhumane housing conditions and other barriers to our contentment. Then, we begin to formulate our personality traits; we begin to hear about stuff like "generational curses." If that wasn't enough, we start to add our own little spices (that are not from God) for a little added flavor. After we become Christians, we set out on this quest to find out what God has destined for our life. This search can go on forever, seemingly going nowhere fast. We begin to seek advice from everyone that we know, trying to get an answer to the question. "What is my destiny?" We eventually realize that God had a plan for our lives before we ever had an opportunity to start "messing it up."

"For those whom He foreknew [of whom He was aware of and loved beforehand]. He also destined from the beginning [foreordaining them] to be modeled into the image of His Son [and share inwardly His likeness], that He might become the firstborn among many brethren."

When You're Tired of Looking Up

Romans 8: 29 Amplified Version

God had a "Manifest Destiny" for our lives from the beginning. He was so gracious to also give us the means to obtain it, but how do we get off course? Do we strap in and hold on for the ride in order to get to our future event that is unavoidable or do we spend our days "looking for destiny in all the wrong places?"

Some years ago, a country music singer wrote a song that described a man looking for love in all the wrong places. The song explains how the singer did everything he could to find a friend and a lover. His search led him to some places that he shouldn't have visited and to some faces that he shouldn't have seen but he kept searching until one day he found the friend and lover he sought after.

After we have gone places we shouldn't have gone and we surely have seen some faces we shouldn't have ever seen, our search leads us right back to Christ, our friend, our lover, our "Manifest Destiny", the future event regarded as unavoidable - a relationship with Jesus Christ our Saviour.

My search to find my destiny began as a young girl trying to find the answer to a laundry list of mysterious sayings that had absolutely no meaning to me at all. My father, who was a Baptist Preacher, told me at a very young age to "just pray and look up." That was the beginning of my journey down a spiraling road of praying and looking up and seeing "nothing". I asked myself more times than I care to mention, "Why am I looking up? Nothing good seems to be *falling into my life." Although I saw nothing, my competitive spirit kept me searching and I thank God that one day I found the answer.*

I thank God for being my "Manifest Destiny" and although I went through a series of changes, He never left me; therefore my future in Him is unavoidable. Believe me, if you keep praying and looking up, you will find that there is a light at the end of the tunnel and it is not a train, but a loving Saviour who made the ultimate sacrifice for us to reach our destiny. Amen!

CHAPTER TWO
JUST PRAY AND LOOK UP

My father, who was the Pastor of the New Zion Baptist Church, taught me to "just pray and look up." Being the obedient child that I was, I did just that, I would pray, make my petition known to God, get up off of my knees and look up! I never asked my father what I was looking for or even why I was looking up; I just did it.

I continued on with my life year after year, situation after situation and problem after problem "just praying and looking up." I stood aimlessly by as I watched people flood the altar with their prayer requests only to be told "honey, just pray and look up." I was well aware that God was in heaven looking down and if I looked up, I'd be reverencing His direction. What was I expecting to really see by looking up? I didn't have a clue, but I looked up from childhood to adolescence, from adolescence to adulthood thinking that somehow the answers would miraculously fall from the sky; although it didn't happen I kept looking anyway.

Because I knew that there had to be more to looking up than just standing in one position with my eyes affixed on the sky, I began to search other places for answers. My search led me to other church members to see if they could help me understand this "looking up" thing, but to my amazement they had received the same information from their parents and grandparents that I had. It appeared as though the whole church was in a quandary but I was determined to keep searching until I solved the mystery of "just pray and keep looking up." My search now led me to other churches, pastors and denominations. I went so far as to consult the Pentecostals and, what we called at that time, the Holiness Church.

This quest for an understanding became my little secret because I was unable to communicate this to my family. They just wouldn't understand. They thought what we had was good enough, but it wasn't enough for me. My little secret finally led me to Pastor Maurice Johnson, Pastor of Johnson Temple Church of God In Christ. Pastor Johnson told me that the reason I couldn't grasp this "looking up" concept was because of a void in my life and that void was a relationship with Jesus Christ. This was total and sheer nonsense. I began to emphatically explain to Pastor Johnson the numerous positions I had held in the church. Apparently he did not understand that I had been in church all of my life. I had not only been a choir member but a choir director, Sunday School Superintendent, Church Treasurer, and please let's not forget Secretary for the Baptist Training Union. How dare he tell ME that I needed a relationship with Jesus Christ? I was appalled.

Pastor Johnson had insulted my upbringing and because of my competitive spirit, I set out to prove him wrong. This relationship thing wouldn't let me go or get away. I was trapped by yet another mysterious statement, "you must have a relationship with Christ." I didn't understand that any more than I understood "just pray and keep looking up." At this point, I wondered if Christianity was just full of pointless clichés that one is supposed to comprehend by osmosis. I was determined not to give up until I had some answers. One night, as I sat on my bed, I told God, "I want more of you and if having this "relationship" with you will give me what I need and fill this desire in my life, then Here I Am!"

CHAPTER THREE
THE SEARCH IS ON!
RUBY LEE TO THE RESCUE

Selling out to Christ wholeheartedly is the best decision I have ever made in my life. However, as we all know, few decisions, especially those for Christ, come without their share of obstacles. I was not exempt. I had my share of troubles, distractions and even confrontations from my family. My family was not confrontational due to their lack of love, but their concern for my well being. They simply could not understand my strong desire to please God.

By this point in my life, I knew what it meant to have a relationship with my parents, my sisters, and my friends, but a real relationship with Christ was something that was extremely foreign to me. So I did the only thing an analytical person would do, I began to read books. I set out to analyze this relationship thing to the fullest extent. I read books on God's relationship with man, God's relationship with women, any book with the words God and relationship in it I bought, read, and analyzed.

Equipped with all this "book knowledge" on Christ and relationships, I approached the most spiritual person I knew at that time, Evangelist Ruby Nelson (Pedescleaux) to confirm all that I had read an analyzed. After listening to my synopsis of how to obtain a "Real relationship with Christ," she looked at me and told me that I'd obtained great "book knowledge" but I had no revelation with my knowledge.

The days of Pastor Maurice Johnson flashed before my eyes. What was the problem now? Not only was I able to give a synopsis of every type of relationship there was with Christ, I was able to quote the scripture that substantiated my claim of obtaining so much knowledge.

> *Study and be eager and do your utmost*
> *To present yourself to God approved (tested by*
> *Trial), a workman who has no cause to be ashamed*
> *Correctly analyzing and accurately dividing*
> *(rightly handling and skillfully teaching)*
> *the Word of truth!*
> *2 Timothy 2:15 (Amplified version)*

Ruby Lee gave me another mysterious statement, just like Pastor Johnson had done. She said, "I had to submit my will to God's will. I had to let go of all the book knowledge and ask God to come into my life and set up residence." Here we go again, another mysterious command that appears to have no instructions on how to obtain it. I had gone from "just pray and look up" to having a "relationship with Christ" and now I have to figure out how to submit my will to God's will. The race was on then. Hmmm, how do I submit my will to God's will and reap His benefits? This was starting to be too much pressure. How was I going to have a relationship with God while my biological family was watching my every move?

When You're Tired of Looking Up

CHAPTER FOUR
HELP, RUBY LEE, HELP!!!!

I found myself once again on a quest for answers. This time I began to spend as much time as possible with Ruby Lee. I would ask questions like "How will I know that I have a relationship with God, when will I know and what will it feel like?" I began to travel with her when she went to preach at other churches. I would even drive her to her preaching engagements if necessary. I was determined that she was the person that was going to help me solve this mystery.

Ruby Lee was a trailblazer. I would set up preaching engagements for her at churches that didn't welcome women preachers with open arms or congregations that just would rather be entertained than taught holy living. She was a woman who had truly solved the mystery of having a relationship with God. I was so determined to grasp this same concept that I spent hours and days just sitting in her presence, allowing her to pour into my spirit wisdom and knowledge. My family never suspected a thing because Ruby Lee was my cousin. Little did they know I was gradually being drawn into a relationship with Christ right before their very eyes and they didn't even see it coming.

Having been raised in the church, I had scripture memorization down to a fine art. Ruby Lee taught me to read God's word without a preconceived conclusion. Okay now we have a real problem and a serious challenge. I now had to go back and read passages of scriptures that I was quite familiar with and allow the Lord to minister to me what He wanted me to know from that particular scripture. Who knew all this was involved in having a relationship with Christ? I was determined, however, to see it through to the end. As time went on she would give me scriptures to read focused upon the control of my finances and living a Holy and acceptable life unto God. The real challenge came when she asked me to fast for a day. She asked me to fast from the time I got up until 6:00PM that evening. I had never heard of such nonsense before in all my life. All I knew about a fast was how fast I could eat my food. I asked her "Are you crazy? Why do I need to not eat in order to spend time with the Lord?" She replied, "It's submission, and your flesh must learn to submit to the Holy Spirit that's within you." I thought this was unnecessary and submitting didn't take all that, but because I trusted her, I went along with the fast. Guess what? Nothing monumental happened in my life that day. All I know is that at 5:45PM I had my plate of food ready to be eaten, at 5:55PM I blessed my food and two seconds after 6:00PM I was enjoying the best meal I'd ever eaten.

When I reported to Ruby Lee that I'd accomplished this assignment, I asked what's next? She said that I needed to begin to ask God to baptize me in the Holy Spirit with the evidence of speaking in tongues. Now mind you, I'd heard her speak in tongues many times while preaching and I had witnessed many people receive the Baptism in the Holy Spirit with the evidence of speaking in tongues, but I felt that if that was what they wanted, all well and good, but I was doing just fine without it.

CHAPTER FIVE
I CAN FEEL THE BREAKING OF DAY

In November 1984, after Ruby Lee had preached a revival at Barksdale Air Force Base, Shreveport, Louisiana, we went out for coffee and she asked if I'd been praying for the Baptism in the Holy Spirit; I told her no. I still firmly believed that it didn't take all of that to have a relationship with Christ. In her best ministry voice she said, "Yes, YOU do need it because if you really want the relationship that you claim and desire with Christ, then YOU, Gladys, need it." I was almost afraid to ask. Here we go again. Reluctantly I asked, "How do I get it?" She said that word again, SUBMIT. I began to wonder, how much more do I need to submit to before I have a relationship with Christ?

My analytical mind began to work once more. Was I supposed to say what I heard other people say when they spoke in tongues? If that was the case, I had a good memory and could repeat what I heard with no mistakes. I was told once more that when I submit my heart, my will and my vocal chords to God, He would bring forth my own personal prayer language.

The next night of the revival, while sitting listening to Ruby Lee minister to people, she called me up to the altar. Now I felt that she had really put me on the spot. Scared and shaking, I made my way up to the front. I looked around to see if there was anyone in the congregation that recognized me or that I would see on the next day. Because of my status in the government workplace, I was not going to be found speaking in tongues or even slain in the Spirit on the floor, not me! I had an image to keep up.

In MY mind, I was going to go along with her by letting her pray for me. Then, I would return to my seat and fuss her out when we got home. I never will forget what happened that night. She stood in front of me, and with a soft voice that I'd never heard from her, she whispered in my ear and said, "Lift your hands and receive from the Lord." She didn't yell or tell me what to say. I lifted my hands and immediately I heard something come out of my mouth that wasn't English. I got scared and shut up. She looked at me, smiled, and said, "You've got it now." When we got home that night, she was excited and wanted to talk about what had happened, but I was afraid that she would tell our family what had happened. I knew that if she told certain members of our family, it would eventually get back to my church family and I would surely get the left foot of fellowship right out of the church. For the next three years, I had to practice my prayer language in the confines of my home. No one in my immediate family knew that I'd received the Baptism in the Holy Spirit.

The Lord knew that I needed to be in an environment that embraced speaking in tongues and that I didn't have the heart or the nerves to leave my church and unite with another church in the same city. In August 1987, my job relocated my children and me to Panama City, Florida. We began to attend church at the base chapel and when I heard the Pastor's wife stand up and begin to speak in tongues, I said, "Thank God, here's a lady I can talk to," Cindy Groomes. After church that day I made an appointment to meet with her for lunch the next day. She was wonderful! As I poured out to her what my life had been about for the past three years, she calmly said, "I know what *you're going through, because I'm the only one who speaks in tongues in the chapel."*

CHAPTER SIX
I'M GONNA BE ALRIGHT NOW
OR
AM I?

Cindy was a seasoned veteran at speaking in tongues and was not ashamed to stand during praise and worship and speak in her prayer language. She was so good that she could give the interpretation also. As time went on many of the ladies in the chapel received the Baptism in the Holy Spirit with the evidence of speaking in tongues. We would get together in our women's fellowship and we would experience the Power of the Lord in our midst as we all prayed in the Spirit.

With this new freedom to use my prayer language freely, many oppositions and problems began to overwhelm my life: My "main man," my father's health was attacked; I had financial struggles; my daughter was rebelling; child support payments were not being approved. When I felt nothing else could possibly go wrong, one of my closest cousins, a Fifth-grade school teacher, was shot twice in front of her class and left for dead by her husband. Then to add insult to injury, my own momma didn't understand and would constantly ask me, "What kinda church is that you've joined and put my grandbabies in?" In the midst of all these obstacles, I was determined not to go back to my former way of Christianhood. At this point I had no other choice but to rely on the word of God to see me through....

We are troubled on every side, yet not distressed; we are perplexed, but not in despair; Persecuted, but not forsaken; cast down, but not destroyed; Always bearing in the body the dying of the Lord Jesus, that the life also of Jesus might be made manifest in our body.
2 Corinthians 4:8-10

Although many years had passed since I heard the words "just pray and keep looking up," I realized that looking up was okay but standing on the word of God and seeing that word manifest itself through me was a phenomenal experience. It wasn't until this point that I realized that I finally had a relationship with God all of my own.

God then revealed something to me that blew my mind. As a child growing up, I didn't need a relationship with God because Rev. Paul Colwell (my daddy) and Iola Colwell (my momma) had a relationship with God that covered me 24-7. Daddy was a very well known man in Alexandria, Louisiana, even to this day. No matter what his daughters ever got into or needed all we had to do was say 'My daddy is Rev. Paul Colwell' and things would immediately change on our behalf. I didn't need the Lord because I had <u>my daddy!</u> My daddy owned his own construction company, pastored a church, owned thirty acres of land, several cars, a horse, a motorcycle and above all, we had the largest house in the community where we lived. Who needs the Lord when you have more than enough material things? It had never dawned on me before now that I had depended on "my family name" to obtain everything I thought I needed. But now I had to depend on the name of Jesus Christ to obtain everything I will ever need.

Although the words were never uttered to us to explain 'just pray and keep looking up', Daddy showed us by his life that God wants us to have the wealth of the land that He's promised us.

When You're Tired of Looking Up

CHAPTER SEVEN
LET'S GET STARTED?

God has set into motion a plan for your destiny.

For I know the thoughts and plans that I have for you, says the Lord, thoughts and plans for welfare and peace and not for evil, to give you hope in your final outcome. Jeremiah 29:11 (Amplified version)

Submitting to God's will requires you to speak God's word to your flesh daily. The definition of submit means to give way to; give up control of oneself. In our natural thinking, we see submit as being weak, allowing others to take advantage of us or just being in a state of dependency. We've all been taught that in order to be respected in the world we must be independent in all things. So submitting to God requires us to look different to the world's way of doing business. The world's way of doing business has gotten us very little. Our proverbial "light at the end of the tunnel" has either grown dim or gone completely out.

Take a moment and lift your hands to the Lord and pray this prayer: "Lord, right here and now come into my life and set up residence that I will know beyond a shadow of a doubt that I have a true and real relationship with you." Now begin to write down on a sheet of paper all the things that you know will cause a division in your relationship with Christ. In case you can't think of any, I'll help you out, Pride, Malice, Lust of the Eye, Lust of the Flesh, Bitterness, and most of all, UNFORGIVNESS. Getting rid of unforgivness will take care of about 50% of your submission to God's will. The rest will begin to fall away as you stay in His Word.

Submitting to God is not a "one time good deal." It is a way of life, a Christ-Centered-Life. As you remind yourself daily that you want more of Christ living in you than you want of yourself, you will begin to see your new Christ-Centered desires begin to manifest in your life. The Godly desires you had as a child growing up will begin to be seen by you and others. God wants to show Himself through us to win others to Him if we would only allow Him to have full control of every fiber of our being.

CHAPTER EIGHT
A PLAN FOR YOUR DESTINY

The 21st Century Churches are moving in the direction of congregations running after prosperity rather than running after a real relationship with Christ. Members are being taught to invest in the stock market, read the Dow Jones ticker tapes, and put together portfolios that would take a broker with 10 years of experience to explain. They're being taught that promotion comes from above (again keep looking up) and never settle for anything less than the best. This is a good thing because we never want to settle for less than God's best for our lives. Members need and desire financial freedom because we are directed to "owe no man nothing" and to leave an inheritance for our children. So don't misinterpret my point, I am all for financial stability, but are we as a church teaching our members the principle thing, which is how to reach our "Manifest Destiny?" Not just reach a desired goal but to reach that "future event regarded as unavoidable," a relationship with Jesus Christ.

You constantly hear that God is able to supply your needs, heal your loved ones, save the lost, and deliver you out of the hands of the enemy.

Sunday after Sunday these messages are bellowed from pulpits all over the world but what happens with the returns that don't yield a profit? How do you continue when the promotions don't come, your loved one dies of an overdose, and it appears nothing is happening for you? Sunday after Sunday you come to church waiting for your "big break" but nothing miraculous seems to happen in your life. Secretly, your faith begins to weaken. You hear testimonies of monetary blessings and your car is sitting outside with no gas in it, and Monday you are going to be evicted from your apartment. You hear how the judge cancelled the sentence of someone else's loved one and your brother gets life with no chance of parole; God healed someone's mother of cancer and yours just went to be with the Lord.

You stand and lift your hands during praise and worship in obedience to what the Pastor has asked you to do. You look up towards heaven and say, "Lord, I Am Tired of Looking Up and nothing seems to be happening for me. Why does it seem that you are blessing people around me who don't even tithe, nor give of themselves as much as I do? Why, Lord, Why? "

I'm going to share with you what God gave me to help me understand this "Why Lord Why?"

When we hear the word of God and allow that word to penetrate our spirits, it begins to grow. Our spirit then wants to be seen, but our soul, which is our mind, our intellect and our emotions gets in the way. When our soul interferes, our body refuses to obey what our spirit man is telling us to do. Look at this illustration.

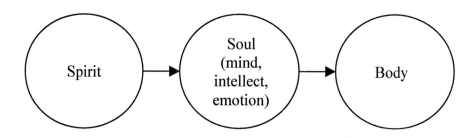

Spirit – word of God is preached and seed is planted. Delight yourself in the Lord and He will give you the desires of your heart,

Psalm 37:4. Good news! In order for your body to react and step out on what God has put into your spirit, it has to pass through your Soulish realm. So on Sunday your spirit is on fire and believing, "I can have what I believe." But then on Monday your Soulish realm says, "No you can't; you were born without and you will never have anything." So the 'Body' will never get the news of what the Spirit man is saying and will cause you to miss out on the promises of God.

It is so important that we understand why we continue to look up and never receive what God has for us. We must not let our Soulish realm distort the message from our Spirit man. It's like waiting on your $10,000.00 tax return and then it's intercepted by a school loan that you owe. You are entitled to the refund, which means that you are entitled to receive the blessing of God. However, you allowed your old way of not paying your bills, your Soulish realm to interfere with your receiving the money that's yours.

Your Spirit man must continue to be fed in order that your Soulish realm can decrease and your Body can get the message from the Spirit man much quicker. How is that done? Take a look at this illustration:

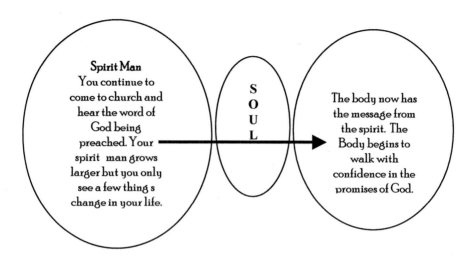

God's Word

Now that the Spirit man is larger than the Soulish realm, the Spirit tells your Soul "You can not control any longer; I'm on a mission to diminish your control forever." So what happens is the Spirit penetrates the Soulish realm on a mission to get the message to the Body so the Body can get busy walking in the promises of God.

For years, many Christians have heard the word of God and worked in many areas of the church. They have been faithful in paying their tithes, they have been dependable and honest. They have prayed for the sick and the sick recovered. They have prayed for the homeless, and watched them become owners of estates. They are viewed by others as Spiritual Giants, but nothing ever seems to happen for them. This could cause a person to wonder why the so-called "Giants" are always broke, never having enough to sustain them from one week to another, and will try and convince others that they don't want anything else from God. All they have ever wanted out of life is to have a relationship with the Lord but say that they do not need the material blessings. In simple terms, **THAT'S A LIE!**

Lest Satan should get an advantage of us; for we are not ignorant of his devices.
2 Corinthians 2:11 (KJV)

To keep Satan from getting the advantage over us; for we are not ignorant of his wiles and intentions.
2 Corinthians 2:11 (Amplified version)

Satan's job description is really simple...steal, kill and destroy. He robs us through our Soulish realms, our minds, our intellects and our emotions. By keeping us in bondage to ourselves, with statements such as "You don't deserve to have ____; what makes you think you're entitled to _____; stop dreaming." When these thoughts are brought to us and we learn to recognize from whence they've come, our Spirit Man should immediately stand tall and command God's word ... "Get thee hence, Satan!"

Be encouraged to know that as your Spirit Man grows that you will not allow your Soulish realm to deprive you of the promises of God because your Body will get the messages a lot quicker.

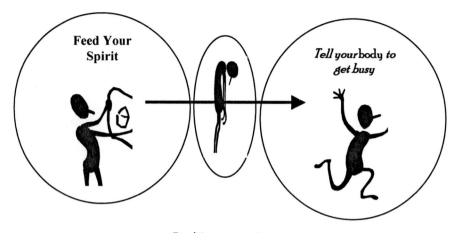

Don't let your soul
control

Your body can't walk in the promises until the Spirit Man pushes the message through your mind. Don't let your mind get in the way of your receiving from God. The cliché, "the mind is a terrible thing to waste," is a true statement because we allow our minds to control our destiny. We either can believe what's been received from our Spirit Man and act upon it, or we can let our minds "kill" every expectation that we have of being blessed by God. Don't waste your mind!

CHAPTER NINE
TELL ME MORE!

So now the question is 'where do I begin?' Start by repenting to God for not believing His Word. You will probably say, 'I do believe God's Word.' This could very well be true, but what part of God's Word do you believe and what part of God's Word do you doubt for your life? We are quick to say that we believe and understand the Word of God, but understanding means comprehension to the point of application. We have been programmed to respond to others when given information or instructions with "I Understand." If we really understood God's Word we would never lack, nor be deprived of His manifold blessings. The Lord will allow us to experience periodic blessings. What I mean by this is that every once in a while God showers us with answers to our prayers that we have prayed. He wants to show us that for the short period of time that we made our request, we didn't let our Soulish realm interfere or come between our Spirit Man and our Body.

We have managed to hit the right notes and chords when our backs are up against a wall. However, why not keep that fervent tenacity going all the time? When things are going well, or should I say when we are comfortable with me, mine these four and no more; we tend not to spend the time communicating with God as we should. Oh, but let a loved one become sick or we have to face some unexpected problem that hits so hard it literally knocks you to your knees and we become relentless in our pursuit to make contact with God. Understanding – Standing Under God's Word brings about a change in our lives that is only for our good. Your heart is changed when you understand God's Word. Without understanding His Word, your faith is fake.

Trust in the Lord with all thine heart; and lean not unto thine own understand. In all thy ways acknowledge Him, and He shall direct thy path.
Proverb 3:5-6 (KJV)

My son, if thou will receive my words and hide my commandments with thee; So that thou incline thin ear unto wisdom, and apply thine heart to understanding; Yea, if thou criest after knowledge, and liftest up thy voice for understanding; If thou seekest her as silver and searchest for her as for hid treasurer, then shalt thou understand the fear of the Lord and find the knowledge of God.
Proverbs 2:1-5 (KJV)

Understanding is the wellspring of life. Ask God to create within you a clean heart and renew a right spirit within you so that you can begin to think differently. Get in front of the mirror and read scriptures to yourself as to how God sees you. Don't be concerned with how your relatives, friends or even church members see you or even how you see yourself. God constantly reminds us to 'get an understanding,' throughout His Word. Understand and <u>Stand Under</u> God's Word as you read it to yourself and feel His anointing begin to fill your spirit and saturate every fiber of your body as you recommit to never walk in defeat again! Stop now, get up and get in the mirror and read these scriptures "with authority" to yourself......

I will praise thee; For I am fearfully and wonderfully made, marvelous are thy works and that my soul knoweth right well...
Psalm 139:14 (KJV)

For I know the thoughts I think toward you saith the Lord, thoughts of peace; and not of evil, to give you an expected end.
Jeremiah 29:11 (KJV)

No weapon that is formed against thee shall prosper; and every tongue that shall rise against thee in judgement thou shalt condemn. This is the heritage of the servants of the Lord, and their righteousness is of me, saith the Lord.
Isaiah 54:17

Keep reading...............don't stop

*This book of the law shall not depart out of your
mouth, but you shall meditate on it day and night,
that you may observe and do according to
all that is written in it. For then you shall make
your way prosperous, and then you shall deal
wisely and have good success.
Joshua 1:8 (Amplified version)*

*Beloved, I wish above all things that
thou mayest prosper and be in health
even as thy soul prospereth.
3 John 2 (KJV)*

Now that you've gained the understanding as to how to receive your inheritance from God by starting with feeding your Spirit Man and then sending the message to your Body through your mind, you can now live the abundant life that God has promised to all those who would but Believe, Understand, Pray and Keep Looking Up To Him!

CHAPTER TEN
THROUGH MANY DANGERS
TOILS AND SNARES

When You're Tired of Looking Up

There's a statement that's used by many Christians in the South, "Child, you see where I am now, but you don't know where I've come from." When I stop and look back (not up this time) I realize that the Lord brought me to where I am the easiest way I'd come. I didn't come to the relationship I have now with the Lord overnight.

> *Through many dangers toils and snares,*
> *I have already come. Twas grace that*
> *brought me safe thus far and grace*
> *will lead me home.*
> *(Amazing Grace)*

Growing up as the 'knee baby' of the family was a blessing. Let me explain what a 'knee baby' is – it's the child that's just older than the baby or next to the baby. I was the third from the oldest and the knee baby; what a great position to be in. I believed that by being the knee baby, I was safe, because if anything happened within the sibling realm, I would never be the one who got blamed. Loved it!

If something got broken in the house, my patent answer was (depending on the size of the object) either 'that baby of yours momma is so bad and she broke it' or 'now momma you know that I'm not big enough to break that thing, must have been one of your older daughters, Dorothy or Ruth.'

Many times I believed that my protection came from being in the middle or from within. Dorothy and Ruth would always be there assuming responsibility and Ann would be there to take the blame.

Gladys Henderson-Williams

Everyone knows that the baby of the family never does anything wrong and will never get the whipping they deserve. This was wonderful growing up, but when we all became adults things changed. Even though all of us were from the same womb with the same father, our desires and dreams were very different. Isn't it amazing how a group of siblings who are raised in the same house, ate from the same table and parented by the same two people can turn out so different in their lives? Ruth, the oldest, was a very strong woman and believed that because she'd taken so much of the blame growing up that in adulthood, she wasn't going to be blamed for anything else that someone did. She was relentless in her pursuit to attain material wealth. If anyone got in her way she would either dismiss them out of her life or treat them as if they didn't exist. Other people would not bother her. She would say, "Don't let people get too close to you." Now if none of the above worked, she would give you an old fashion cussing that would put a sailor to shame; she was good. I loved and admired her inner strength.

I watched her one day as she packed her belongings and said, "I'm moving to Los Angeles, California." I remember being scared for her going alone but she was determined to travel and see more of the world. After five years in California she decided to move to Houston, Texas and later moved back to Alexandria, Louisiana. I would always say, "I wanted so much to be like Ruth, not afraid to leave home and see the world." At the age of 48 she was diagnosed with a rare heart disease and went to be with the Lord February 18, 1991, age 49.

When You're Tired of Looking Up

The best friend I had in the 'whole-wide-world' was my sister Dorothy. She was two years older than I was so we spent a lot of time growing up together and sharing secrets that momma and daddy never knew. If one of us got sick, within a day or so, the other one would get sick and this continued even into our adulthood. Dorothy was a very quiet natured person, until you really pushed the envelope with her and then she would retaliate. She took whippings for me because she would always say that I was too skinny to survive one. Daddy rarely whipped us, but the little Creole lady, Iola, would hit you with whatever she had in her hand(s). Dorothy could stand and listen to Daddy fuss about something for a long period of time and it never fazed her. We would ask to borrow the car and daddy would issue specific instructions on how to drive the car. He would tell us how much gas was expected to be in it when it was returned, don't go here, do go there, just a bunch of rules. She would just listen because when he finished his sermon, she knew that she would get the keys and that was her objective. Whereas for me, when he would start issuing out all these rules, after the second rule, my response was "Just forget it, I'll stay home." So for years I longed to have the willpower that she had to keep quiet. And I still haven't mastered that yet!

When I began to move from state to state, promotion after promotion, Dorothy would quit her job and move with me and my children. She would take care of them, get them in school and learn the city while I got us settled in a home and got settled at work. From Panama City, Florida to Denver, Colorado to Hampton, Virginia she was there for me. In Hampton, Virginia was where Dorothy decided to move out of the house with us and get her own apartment. That's when her life took a turn for the worst. She got involved in the drug scene and was found dead lying across her bed of an overdose of Heroin.

    I never will forget the day, October 10, 1997, when I got the news of her death. I was working on a major project for the Department of Defense on an island that sits in the middle of the Atlantic Ocean - an Air Base called Lajes Field, Azores, Portugal. The team that I was in charge of had invited me to watch a movie, Jerry McGuire, and while watching the movie I felt the building begin to shake from a small earthquake. I immediately sensed the urgency to call home and when I did, my husband, Andrew asked, "Where are you? Are you someplace that you can sit down?" I asked why and he said, "Dorothy was found dead lying across her bed in a rooming house." The first thing that came out of my mouth was, "Not my sister Dorothy," and he began to fill me in on the information the Newport News, Virginia Police had given him. Because I was on a military base, the Red Cross got in touch with the Chaplain and the Commander for them to notify me. The island that I was on did not have a commercial airport, and planes didn't fly back to the United States daily, but the next plane that would be going to the states was coming the next day. The news of my being able to leave sounded good. I was thankful that I was going to be able to get home so soon. However, the plane that was supposed to stop and pick me up couldn't land because of the wind blowing over 80mph and the next plane going to the United States wasn't due to come through headed for the states for the next three days.

I couldn't believe this was happening to me. The pain was so great that it hurt to walk, breathe or even think and even now when I think about it – it still hurts (not as much). Here's what I couldn't believe....

- That God would take her from me without letting me know.
- That God would take her from me and me not be in the same city.
- That God would take the best friend that I'd ever had.
- That God claimed that he loved me but would do something like this to me.
- That God didn't even allow me to speak with her before He took her.
- That God knew this would be the greatest pain I'd ever experience and he didn't seem to care.
- That God would have my 77 year old momma bury her second born child.
- That God would leave me here to take care of my momma as the oldest child.
- That the God that I'd bragged about to others on how good, loving and kind He was, didn't seem to love me at all.

- *Most of all I couldn't believe that He ever loved or cared for me at all....*

While walking around that Air Base, I asked God if He even remembered that I had witnessed to others about Him? Didn't He remember how I had led many to Him for salvation? Had He forgotten that I had taught Bible Studies? Had all the things such as how I could be counted on by the ministry to be in place serving wherever needed; how I had tithed faithfully since I was a child; how I had honored my father and my mother; how I had fasted and prayed for others; how I had visited the sick (I even sat with the bereaved); how I would lift my hands and worship Him and this is what I get for serving in the Kingdom — had all of this counted for nothing? **I was ANGRY!**

When You're Tired of Looking Up

CHAPTER ELEVEN
SUFFERING IN SILENCE

When I finally got back to the United States, no one knew that in my heart that I'd given up on believing that lifting my hands and looking up to God was worth doing anymore. Our family got through the funeral with great support from our pastor, Pastor Gerard Ruff, and the Cornerstone Assemblies of God church family. I continued to go to church each Sunday and Bible Study every Wednesday. Two weeks after the funeral, our Annual Women's Conference was held. Since I was the president of the Women's Department, I was so busy being busy, nobody noticed anything different about me. When it came time for praise and worship I found some type of task that needed to be done there so I wouldn't have to stand in the midst of the crowd and participate. Going to church each Sunday became a chore and a burden. I couldn't stay home because people would ask my family 'Where's Gladys?' Being the faithful attendant that I was, I couldn't dare cause or bring any attention to what I was really going through.

Isn't it amazing how we can fool other church members? I would go to church and when the Pastor would ask everyone to lift their hands and look to the hills from whence cometh your help, I'd participate physically, but my heart was nowhere in the place. I would stand there with my hands raised, tilt my head back, and look at the weather out of the window that is at the top of the church building. This continued for at least three or four months.

Finally, one Sunday when corporate praise and worship was going forth, and no one was paying attention to me (I thought) I let my hands down and must have had the meanest look on my face.

Pastor Lena Mae Alston, one of the pastors of the church, saw the look. I was Busted! All I knew to do at that point was get out of there. When I walked in the fellowship hall to exit the church, she grabbed my arm, looked me dead in my eyes and said, "Do you know what your problem is?" I stood there looking at her wishing she would just let go of me before I gave her a problem. She said, "You are mad with God because you feel like God took your sister away from you. She was never yours in the first place. She belonged to God, just like you." If there was ever a word to describe mad to the tenth power...then that's what I was. Mad to the tenth power!

I felt that my heart could not and would not ever heal. I knew Dorothy was using drugs but she never used them around me. She was only 45 years old. God could have cleaned her up and won her to Him. I kept doing the routine things in the church so no one would question my absence.

The amazing thing about being in corporate worship is that you can only stay so long without it penetrating your Spirit Man. When you have to sit and listen to the preached word, because the ushers halt the walking during the sermon, your Spirit Man is being filled and you're none the wiser.

Several times I found myself clapping my hands in honest praise but when I realized that I was supposed to be mad with God, I would immediately stop. I wanted God to feel the pain I felt and I didn't know of any other way to get my point across to Him. I know many Spiritual Giants who would have kicked me out of the church if I'd

Gladys Henderson-Williams

told them that I was mad with God. I wasn't upset...I was mad and there was one thing for sure, God knew I was mad.

When You're Tired of Looking Up

CHAPTER TWELVE
A New Day is Dawning

In January 1998, Pastor Ruff called for a week of fasting and praying. It was during this week, of fasting from 6:00 AM till 6:00PM and praying nightly for 7:00PM– 8:00PM, that Pastor Ruff asked if there was anyone who had been holding a grudge of any sort to please come up for prayer. He said it didn't matter who the grudge was against your boss, husband, wife, children, co-workers, siblings and especially if you were angry with God about something.

I wanted to go up for prayer, but pride wouldn't let me go. I felt that if I went up to the front, I would probably lose my composure and just fall to the floor and scream for hours. So I didn't go that night. The next night I just knew he wouldn't make the same plea again. Guess what? He did. My daughter came behind me and said, "Ma I'm not letting you go out like this. You're trying to die because your sister is gone and you are mad with God. Ma, you need to let it go." She took me to the altar and to the very pastor who had peeped my hold card.

I went out of obedience to my daughter, thinking that I'd get one of those two minute prayers. To my amazement, Pastor Alston, the same person who had confronted me earlier about my sister, got the anointing oil and put enough oil on me to fry a chicken! What she said to me that day, I will never forget; she said, "Lift your hands." I put them up a little, she said, "I mean high." So I went a little higher; she said, "that's not high enough, stretch them to the ceiling," and I did. The release I felt resembled the pressure being released off a radiator cap of a car when it's hot. A loud yell came up from my belly that I'd never heard before. It felt like someone was pulling grass out by the roots. It hurt!

I stood there for quite a while before I could gain my composure. This time when I lifted my hands, and looked to heaven something good did fall into my life. I had totally surrendered every fiber of my body back to God. I didn't allow the Soulish realm to interfere because what I needed from God on that day I was determined to get and nothing or nobody was going to stop me. Peace fell, joy fell, revelation knowledge fell, blessings fell and many, many more good things. As a result of that experience I began to see and witness the manifestation of God as never before. That day was the beginning of a new life for my family and me.

What I hadn't realized or acknowledged was that I had literally put my family through pure hell with my bad attitude. My attitude was so bad that no one in the house wanted to be around me. I was so bitter. I could find something wrong with you just looking at me and smiling. I would do the 'church thing' smile, shake hands, and may even issue out a few hugs on my way to my car. I would always say to the congregants that 'You know I'm always busy, so I gotta go' and they never questioned me. God forbid if I accidentally crossed paths with our Senior Pastor Ruff, I'd immediately start a conversation about something insignificant that I could quickly end. I could see that my Pastor wanted me to talk but the devil had me to believe that 'No One Understood or Cared!'

CHAPTER THIRTEEN
MY BLESSING

Before I continue I must back up a little, in 1994 the Lord sent a man into my life, Andrew Jonathan Williams Sr. Andrew was the man that God had tailor-made for me because He knew what I'd be facing in 1997. I didn't understand why the Lord was sending someone into my life when I already had everything I needed. I had momma living with me since my daddy died in 1990; I had a great job that paid me very well; I was a member of a great church. I even had one or two close friends, my children were healthy and happy, but most of all I had <u>Dorothy.</u> The song says, "Who could ask for anything more?" I couldn't think of another thing to add to my list of wants.

I walked around saying, "Destiny has arrived for me." I had no problem with Andrew being a friend or a business associate. I felt he was the greatest trainer in the Financial Services Business and I admired that, but nothing more. Because I had been married before, I figured that part of the reason that my marriage didn't work was because I never asked God to teach me to be a good wife. I'd always asked the Lord to be a good daughter to my parents and a good mother to my children. Asking the Lord to be a good wife or even a half-way good wife was never on my prayer request list because it didn't matter. I believed that as long as I had the people who were most important to me, with me then nothing else mattered. Since Andrew was a member of the church also, I would see him on Sundays and Wednesdays, coming to church with his son and daughter. I had seen him around prior to 1994, but it hadn't really mattered. Something happened prior to the Lord sending him to me for me. My daughter got pregnant her senior year in high school (that's another 500 page book) and 96% of her church friends stopped associating with her. She would always tell me that "The man, who plays the trumpet, always encourages me to keep my head up." Before I knew it, she was calling him 'Uncle Drew.' He was the first uncle she'd ever had and the relationship posed no threat to me.

I went to him one Sunday and said, "Thanks for encouraging my daughter." From that point we would exchange greetings and be on our way if there was no business to discuss.

During this time in my life, I was traveling with my job 80% of the year. It was not a problem, remember? I had Momma and Dorothy to take care of any and every thing with my children that they needed. I could travel and stay weeks at a time if necessary.

On April 3, 1994, Andrew invited me out for a cup of coffee at I-Hop. Everyone that knows me, knows that if you mention a cup of coffee, I'm there. He knew that I had a flight to catch the next morning at 6:30AM to go to New Jersey to work. We sat in I-Hop drinking coffee and talking until I had only enough time to get home, pack, and get to the airport. He was such a gentleman that he gave me a ride to the airport.

Two days later, one of my two close friends, Bobby Runion, had died in his sleep. Bobby was an epileptic and I had helped him face many challenges during his time in the military. When I got the call from our pastor, telling me of Bobby's death, I came home to help his family with the arrangements. It was then that I called Andrew and told him Bobby had died. He said, "Life is just so short." Little did I realize that as God had taken one of my friends, He was sending the man into my life who would become my "bestest friend." The Lord told Andrew that I would be his wife and he told the Lord "Not Sis. Henderson, she's mean." What he meant was that from the time I first met him, he would tease my friend Doris and me about finding us husbands. Doris and I would hang out together when I was in town. We would go out and drink coffee late at night. My answer to Andrew would always be, "Doris may want one, but I certainly don't want a husband"

The day that Andrew told me what the Lord had said about my becoming his wife, guess where I went? To find Dorothy! Dorothy had to hear everything. I couldn't do anything without her approval. I knew that God's approval was good but Dorothy's approval was good too. I took her to meet Andrew and she said 'He is a great guy, gurl.' Andrew would propose to me at least 10 times a day because we talked 10 times a day. During this time, I was working in Denver, Colorado, and my answer would be, "No!"

Then finally God's plan overruled my plan. I came home for a visit, we purchased the license, and forty-five days from the cup of coffee at I-Hop we were married. Thank God for my Blessing!!!!

God was setting things in order for what was going to happen in 1997 and I didn't realize it. Now, Pastor Andrew Jonathan Williams is a wonderful husband, father to all our children, daddy, pops and grandpa. God knew that Andrew was the only man that would walk with me through the hardest thing that I'd have to go through in 1997. He comforted me, wiped many tears, confirmed that it was Dorothy that was found, and he let me vent. Always praying for me, holding *me saying, "It will be all right, hang in there." When I couldn't sleep, he would sit up with me. God gave him the words to say because God knew the hurt that I felt. He's a Godsend...*

CHAPTER FOURTEEN
MANIFEST DESTINY

Since that encounter with God at the altar, I've still had many challenges in my life, but through continuous prayer, Bible study, fasting and reading God's Word - I finally understand the formula to walking in the promises of God. He allowed me to go through the valley in order for me to get my priorities in line with what His will was for my life. The Lord delivered me and set me free from me. He restored the years that I allowed the cankerworm and locust to eat away and now I walk in His promises. HALLELUJAH!!! I'm now able to stand and proclaim God's Word to others - that it's your inheritance to have His choice blessings. Daily I ask God to prepare and give me the opportunity to witness to others the things He's done for me.

****

Now that I understand………this is my practice.

When obstacles of any sort, big or small, wide or deep, attempt to rob me of my joy, I reflect back on the illustrations in the previous chapters and realize that I must keep my Soulish realm under the authority that God has given me. Paul said, "I press forth to the mark of a high calling," so I bear down and call forth my Spirit Man and command Him to stand tall as we take this message from the Spirit through the Soulish realm to my Body so I can run with confidence the race that God has set before me and reach the Destiny that God put in place for me before the foundation of the World. With the anointing that God has placed on my life, I commission you to apply the word of God as written in Romans 12:1 (KJV)

> *I beseech you therefore, brethren, by the mercies of God, that ye present your bodies a living sacrifice, holy, acceptable unto God which is your reasonable service.*

Things in your life will not change overnight, however when situations and problems come your way, you now have the Understanding how to handle them. I join with you now as you stand, lift your hands and look up and with the power and authority that God has given you, knowing beyond a shadow of a doubt that Good things, Good Success is coming to you and your household. Now watch God manifest manifold blessing in your life so much so that blessing will begin to overtake you. Just as in Malachi 3:10b 'there shall not be room enough to receive them all.' Amen

EPILOGUE

*For I know the thoughts that I think towards you,
Saith the Lord, thoughts of peace and not
Of evil, to give you an expected end.
Jeremiah 29:11*

God truly does have a destiny for our lives. I encourage you to apply the principles that God has given me to share with you and watch God move in your life. Once we get our priorities straight and realize that it is not the acquisition of goods that determines our destiny but the fact that we have a relationship with a loving God. A God that loved us so much that He sacrificed His most prized possession, His Son. A God who doesn't leave you while you to go through everything you go through.

As I went through all the things in my life, as well as inflicting some discomfort on a few people along the way, I have come to realize that God's steadfast love is never ending. His mercies are new every morning—Great is His Faithfulness.

If you are a parent, teach your children at an early age the formula to receive all the blessings of God. Witness to everyone you come in contact with because one of them just might be a relative of mine and I would appreciate your helping me see my entire family in Heaven.

I thank God that, although it took me a while, I have learned to have a real relationship with Him. Now I watch my children as they have their own quest for a relationship with Christ. They are not afraid to walk in the promises of God because they have been taught not to let the Soulish realm hinder them from having what God says they can have. They are not ashamed of the Gospel of Jesus Christ because they know the power and affect He has on others. If this can happen in my life, after all I've been through, it can surely happen in yours.

Regardless of what your beginnings were, God has a *"future event regarded as unavoidable"* for your *"Manifest Destiny."*

Therefore if any man be in Christ, he is a new
Creature; old things are passed away
Behold all things become new.
2 Corinthians 5:17

The ultimate *"Manifest Destiny"* for every believer is to reign with God forever; for He promised if we suffer with Him we will reign with Him
(Live forever in His Presence).
OUR FUTURE EVENTS REGARDED AS UNAVOIDABLE!

Thank You Jesus
Praise God

About the Author

A native of Alexandria, Louisiana, Gladys Henderson-Williams, is the third child born to Rev. Paul and Iola Colwell. She accepted Christ into her life at the age of ten. Gladys was diagnosed with asthma at the age of six, but also was taught that prayer could deliver her from this chronic illness and she was healed. Growing up in the church, she has held many positions in the church, from Sunday School Secretary, Baptist Training Union Secretary, Sunday School Teacher and Choir Director. She was a born leader with great vision who wanted to exceed the expectation that her parents had set for her….a degree and a good paying job.

With her parent's expectations before her, Gladys set out on a journey to make her parents proud. Since she left the starting gate, she has received many, many awards of recognitions from her occupation as a Mission Support Accountant for the Department of Defense to Sunday School Teacher of the Year. Her heart's desire is to see the lost saved and the sick healed. From talking about Christ in the Pentagon to the streets in the inner city, Gladys has never been afraid of letting anyone know that her faith in Christ has been the driver behind all of her accomplishments.

Gladys serves the Lord in the capacity of the Women's Ministry President/Coordinator and a member of the Finance Committee at Cornerstone Assembly of God Church, Hampton, VA. Gladys strives for excellence in doing the will of the Lord. Her favorite pastime is reading and the scripture she lives by daily is Philippians 2:3, "Let nothing be done through selfish ambition or conceit, but in lowliness of mind, let each esteem others better than himself."

She currently resides in Hampton, VA with her husband, Andrew Williams Sr.

Printed in the United States
1438500005B/487-597